ARTILLERY

ARTILLERY

by John Nicholas

Rourke Enterprises, Inc.
Vero Beach, Florida 32964

Since the dawn of mechanized warfare, big guns and heavy howitzers have been the major instrument of force for smashing up enemy positions and destroying field units.

Library of Congress Cataloging-in-Publication Data

Nicholas, John, 1944-
    Artillery/by John Nicholas.
    p. cm. — (The Army library)
    Includes index.
    Summary: Describes the various types of artillery used by the United States Army during different times in history, including self-propelled howitzers, light artillery, towed heavyweights, and other kinds of guns.
    ISBN 0-86592-419-8
    1. United States. Army — Artillery — Juvenile literature.
[1. United States. Army — Artillery. 2. Artillery.] I. Title.
II. Series: Nicholas, John, 1944- Army library.
UF23.N53   1989   88-32726
358'.12 - dc19   CIP
                                  AC

CONTENTS

THE BIG GUN

For several thousand years, war was fought between armies equipped with cavalry, foot soldiers, and **artillery**. After World War One ended in 1918, the horse-mounted soldier gave way to tanks and armored fighting vehicles and later to helicopter gunships that appeared with the **Vietnam War**. The artillery was provided first by men with bows and arrows, then with rifles and cast-iron cannons, and now with big guns and **howitzers**.

The age of machine warfare arrived in about 1916, when big guns appeared during World War One. Before that, cannons and howitzers were much the same as they had been for two hundred years. A cannon is a gun that sends a shell along the barrel at high speed to hit a target at great velocity. Velocity measures how the speed of an object changes with distance. High velocity means an object has high acceleration.

A howitzer is a cannon, or big gun, with a relatively short barrel and a low shell velocity. The shell is the charge that is fired from the barrel, and the diameter of the inside of the barrel, expressed in inches or millimeters, is said to be the **caliber**. A caliber of 75mm describes the barrel's internal diameter (75mm is almost 3 inches). Before World War One, the British used standard English measurements of inches, feet, and yards. The countries on the continent of Europe, such as France, Belgium, and Germany, expressed measurement in metric units of millimeters, centimeters, or meters.

For more than 150 years, artillery has been vital to an army's ability to fight and win battles.

In 1917 the Germans built Big Bertha, one of the biggest guns ever constructed, with a barrel 112 feet long and a weight of 138 tons.

M. G. 3 f.

The gun was attached to a test stand for firing trials and later mounted on a huge rail car for operational use.

Barrel length is sometimes measured in calibers. For instance, a 75mm gun may be described as a 30-caliber gun. In this case the actual barrel length is 2,250mm, or 30 times 75. A British gun of 1914 had a caliber of 3.3 inches and its barrel was 28 calibers, or 92.4 inches in length. This gun could fire an 18-pound charge a maximum range of about four miles.

Some guns were mounted on axles with two or four wheels. This type was a legacy of the old gun carriages drawn by horses. Horses were still used in World War One to drag guns, but the idea of the quick charge across a cavalry-filled battlefield had been replaced by lines of artillery pieces (guns, cannons, or howitzers) set up in the front line of battle to pound enemy defenses with what artillerymen call a barrage.

World War One saw some of the most horrifying barrages of all time. One eyewitness said the guns were "like a gigantic forge that never stopped pounding, day or night." It reached a peak in 1916, when British and French guns were set up for the most enormous barrage ever known. The goal was to kill German troops cowering in

The gun assembly and its support cradle had a total weight of 256 tons.

trenches along a five-mile front and thus clear the way for an infantry advance. In seven days, more than 1,500 guns fired two million shells without pause. That is an average of more than 200 shells every minute continuously for one week. Each gun fired almost 1,300 shells.

The biggest and most powerful gun of World War One was the appropriately named "Big Bertha," built by the Germans in 1917. Its barrel was 112 feet long, its caliber 381mm, and it weighed 138 tons. The gun was mounted on an enormous rail car, and the complete assembly had a total weight of 256 tons. It was built to bombard Paris, and on March 23, 1918, it began a terrifying series of firings. They lasted until the Germans retreated, taking their gun with them, almost five months later. In that period they fired 367 shells, killed 256, and wounded 620 people of Paris.

Whenever the gun was fired, the shell left the **muzzle**, the front end of the gun barrel, at a velocity of 5,260 feet per second (more than 3,500 MPH). After 90 seconds, the shell had climbed to an altitude of 24 miles, reached the top of its arching trajectory, and begun its downward path to the center of Paris, almost 70 miles from where it had been fired. The shell struck the ground at a speed of more than 2,000 MPH.

World War One artillery proved the vulnerability of infantry by pounding them to death in the millions; more than ten million soldiers were killed between 1914 and 1918, largely as a result of artillery bombardment. On the first day of the Battle of the Somme in July 1916, more than 57,000 British soldiers lost their lives to gunfire. In terms of what it achieved during World War One, the wholesale use of artillery was human slaughter on a massive scale.

When the war ended in 1918, military forces were disbanded and there were few developments in warfare for about ten years. Then with improvements to motor-driven vehicles and an emphasis on tanks moving quickly across the battlefield, thoughts turned again to the big guns. Instead of armies digging trenches and blasting each other from fixed positions, troops in the future could fight mobile wars across large areas. This meant the artillery would have to move, too, and keep pace with the advancing front of the battlefield.

Today, all artillery like the Soviet 152mm howitzer must be highly mobile and designed to be carried by fast-moving armies. ▼

Big Bertha was used to bombard Paris almost seventy miles away; the shells hit the ground at more than 2,000 MPH.

One way of moving the artillery was to couple guns to trucks and other vehicles that had been adapted with tracks, enabling them to pull heavy artillery across rough country. During World War Two (1939-45), the Germans began to use **self-propelled artillery**. Self-propelled guns looked like tanks with fixed guns on top instead of moving turrets. The development of tanks had led to the development of self-propelled artillery. With these, artillery could move quickly and keep up with the advancing tanks and infantry.

The gun and the tracked vehicle have been combined into a new class of self-propelled artillery for the battlefield.

World War Two also saw the return of the big howitzers, although none had the range of Big Bertha. One of the biggest howitzers ever built was the American "Little David," which had a 914mm caliber barrel. It was completed in 1945 but the war ended before it could be used. In 1945, the U.S. Army's range of self-propelled guns were mostly 100mm and 155mm, although the T92 howitzer had a caliber of 240mm.

These self-propelled guns were not completely independent, and several other vehicles were required to support their needs, bringing up more shells and supplies. Despite this, the big gun and the self-propelled howitzers were capable of hitting distant targets with enormous firepower totally beyond the range of tanks and other heavy guns, although towed artillery continued to play a useful part.

Light artillery forms an important part of the modern army because it keeps the troops supplied with fire power for an advance across land.

13

LIGHT ARTILLERY

Seen here on a field training exercise, the M101 is one of the oldest weapons still in use with the U.S. Army. It was designed more than sixty years ago and has been in service since 1939.

One of the oldest weapons still in service with the U.S. Army is the M101 105mm howitzer. It dates back to a decision made in 1919 to develop a gun with a 105mm caliber capable of hitting targets more than six miles away. The gun was to be towed by a vehicle and fire a shell weighing about 30 pounds. By 1928 the gun had been designed, and competing proposals from different contractors had been examined. The M101 finally went into production during 1939, the year conflict broke out in Europe.

Before World War Two began, changes had been made to both the M101 and its carriage. The carriage is the supporting frame to which the gun is attached. This includes the axle, wheels, and the split trail. The trail is the combination of one or two arms by which the gun is towed behind a vehicle. In most artillery pieces the trail is split into two sections. When the gun is towed the twin trails are brought together and attached to the vehicle tow bar. When set down on the ground for firing, the split trail is separated and helps keep the gun firmly positioned.

After the war the gun was modified further, with changes to the carriage as well. It remained, however, essentially the same as it was when first placed in production. Production ended in 1953, but the M101 is probably the most widely exported weapon in history. Almost fifty countries operated or still operate this gun, and about 12,000 were eventually built. The M101 weighs less than 5,000 pounds and can fire 8 rounds in the first 30 seconds. It then slows down, because rapid firing heats the gun and prevents it from maintaining a high rate. It can keep up 3 rounds per minute for one hour or more. The M101 has a range of nine miles with rocket-assisted charges.

The M101 shown in this picture and the M102 shown on the next page are the U.S. Army's only 105mm weapons.

Today, about 300 M101s are still in service with the army, but most were replaced by the M102. Designed as recently as the 1950s, the M102 is the only other 105mm towed gun in army use. It was first used in combat in Vietnam in February 1964. The M102 was specifically designed for air transportation and was much lighter than the M101 of a similar caliber. The gun took advantage of many important developments between the 1930s, when the M101 was first produced, and the 1960s. The gun was lower and therefore more difficult for enemy gunners to hit. It had slightly greater range and was easier to move around to change the direction of fire.

The M102 is capable of firing ten rounds per minute, and with rocket-assisted shells the gun has a range of more than nine miles. ▼

The M102 weighs only 3,400 pounds and can fire 10 rounds per minute for long periods. With **rocket-assisted shells**, the gun has a range of more than nine miles and an accurate fire control system. Fire control systems have telescopes and special alignment devices that give information about how to precisely aim the barrel of the gun. The fire control equipment of a gun is vital because no matter how powerfully or rapidly it can fire, if the gunner cannot aim it accurately at the target the weapon is of little use on the battlefield.

The M101 and the M102 are the army's only 105mm weapons. About 1,100 are in use, and 800 of these are the more advanced M102. Collectively, the 105mm-caliber towed guns represent about 19 percent of the total inventory of towed and self-propelled artillery operated by the United States. Guns of this type are highly mobile, can be moved quickly from one place to another, and are sufficiently small and lightweight to make them readily transported by air. They serve a useful purpose as short-range artillery in support of infantry operations.

Most light artillery pieces are designed to provide fire power for troops in the field. The U.S. Army has developed a new gun to support light infantry divisions.

Soviet light artillery pieces match the same requirements as those of the U.S. Army; the Russians have several thousand guns of this type in service. ▲

To replace the M101, the army is buying the M119, a light towed howitzer with a 105mm gun. It has the range of the M102 and with rocket-boosted shells will reach targets twelve miles away. The need for the M119 arose when the army developed a new light infantry division. It is intended to provide a rapid firepower to support troops on the battlefield.

The M119 was designed and developed by the British, who labeled it the L119 during the 1970s. It was one of four **NATO** guns received by the U.S. Army. Buying existing equipment was more economical than going to the expense of a completely new weapon. The L119 showed good performance in the Falklands campaign during 1982. In that conflict, Argentinian armed forces invaded the Falkland Islands, and British troops were sent to liberate them. The L119 consistently outgunned the opposition.

Light guns like this are frequently used as anti-aircraft weapons. ▶

TOWED HEAVYWEIGHTS

Infantry and cavalry divisions are supported by light and medium towed artillery pieces, and guns like this are increasingly important for operations.

The standard 155mm howitzer in service with the U.S. Army between 1920 and 1941 was the French M1917, built in America under a special license. It was so old that special modifications had to be made so that vehicles, rather than horses, could tow it. Its replacement was the M114, which saw extensive service in World War Two, Korea, and Vietnam. By the time production ended, just over 6,000 had been built. Immediately after World War Two the M114 was designated as the army's standard medium-towed howitzer. It eventually served with the armies of 37 countries.

Before the gun is fired, it is raised up on a special firing jack mounted beneath the carriage. The wheels are free of the ground, and split trails help stabilize the gun. The 155mm gun can fire 95-pound shells a distance of nine miles, and a special barrel now being fitted to it will increase this to twelve miles. The standard gun has a continuous rate of fire of 60 shells per hour, and the barrel can fire 7,500 rounds before replacement.

The M114 weighs 12,800 pounds. It can be lifted by a Boeing CH-47 Chinook helicopter, or it can be towed by several different vehicles. So far, about 4,700 M114s have been built, and about 220 are still in service with the U.S. Army. Many more are in service with foreign armies. The M114 can fire a wide variety of shells, including high-explosive, chemical or nuclear. Chemical shells would spread chemical agents on the enemy, causing breathing problems. Nuclear weapons would be used to blast heavily protected, reinforced structures or underground bunkers.

Troops deploy on the island of Grenada in a support operation to prevent a political takeover.

The largest 155mm towed howitzer is the M198, of which the army currently has about 1,000 in use. An additional 1,500 are on order for foreign customers. Development of the gun began in 1968 when a decision was made to replace the standard M114. A special range of ammunition was being developed for long range and high firepower. Some people were concerned that a comparatively light towed gun would not be stable when firing this longer range ammunition.

During trials where more than 45,000 rounds were fired by ten test guns, performance was high. The gun was ordered into production during 1978. The M198 was developed as the standardized 155mm army towed howitzer for general support. The gun is not as mobile as some army generals had hoped, and mobility has been sacrificed for range and high firepower. Deployment of the M198 has now run into serious obstacles, and some senior officers criticize the weapon. Some of their arguments make sense.

◀ With a 155mm gun, the M114 weighs more than 6 tons and can fire 95-pound shells a distance of nine miles.

This giant 8-inch howitzer was developed after World War Two. It is capable of firing a 200-pound shell almost eleven miles.

For one thing, the M198 is too wide to fit on parachute extraction rails in the C-130 Hercules transport plane. Extraction rails are attached to the floor of the cargo plane so cargo on special pallets can be dropped through the rear doors as the plane makes a low pass across the ground. In this way, army equipment can be dropped to troops on the ground without the plane actually landing. As soon as the cargo pallet clears the plane, a parachute is released that helps to slow down and reduce the force of impact with the ground. The M198 is capable of being airlifted by the Boeing CH-47 Chinook helicopter. The 5-ton truck necessary to tow the gun, however, cannot be lifted by the Chinook!

Nevertheless, the M198 is a useful support gun. It does require about eleven men to set up, but it takes less than five minutes to get ready for action or break down for transportation. When firing, accuracy has been generally better than expected and the gun has given good service in the time since it first joined army units in 1978. It is deployed in battalions of 18 guns, with each battalion having three batteries with six guns. Like many defense projects and weapon developments, however, it has seen its fair share of cost escalation. Originally priced at $184,000, each M198 is now coming out at more than $500,000.

The M198 weighs 15,800 pounds and has an overall length of 41 feet and a barrel length of 20 feet. Its 155mm gun can fire a wide variety of shells, including high-explosive, anti-tank mines, grenade canisters of up to 88 grenades per round, smoke bombs, chemical weapons, illuminating shells, or nuclear weapons. Anti-tank mines are dropped by separating the two halves of a canister in flight so that the mines spray out and fall to earth across a wide area. Grenade canisters contain individual grenades that are armed when they fall from the canister in which they were fired. Illuminating shells burn brightly as they slowly descend, lighting up large areas of the enemy positions.

The 155mm M198 is a fine weapon on the battlefield but lacks mobility because it cannot fit inside the commonly used C-130 ▶ *Hercules transport plane.*

A typical M198 gun team includes eleven men and takes less than five minutes to set up for action.

The M198 weighs just over 7 tons and can fire a very wide range of shells, mines, grenades, and chemical or nuclear bombs.

At a sustained rate, the M198 can fire 120 rounds per hour. Standard shells have a range of more than thirteen miles, and special rocket-assisted projectiles give the M198 a range of almost nineteen miles. At this distance, the gun has repeatedly demonstrated it can put the first rounds fired to within 300 feet of the target — an incredible performance. Under short periods of high rates of fire, the M198 can fire four rounds per minute for three minutes, equivalent to one shell every fifteen seconds.

The very latest ammunition for the M198 gives the gun an anti-tank role. With the Copperhead anti-armor munition, the gun uses a special laser beam to pinpoint individual targets and fire precisely and accurately. Accuracy is only good at short range, however, and becomes much less precise at extreme range. The army is interested in developing a new version of the M198 that can be lifted by the latest Sikorsky Black Hawk helicopter. That development may take a long while, though, and the M198 in its standard layout has a very long life ahead.

Firing trials have shown that gun crews are able to maintain a rate of fire equivalent to about 120 rounds per hour.

With the M198 replacing the M101, and the M114 providing medium firepower, the U.S. Army has good artillery for supporting battlefield operations, with troops and **armored personnel carriers** bringing infantry up to the front line. The M198 provides rapid rates of fire for longer distances where fixed firing positions are ensured. The really heavy punch, however, can never be provided by towed guns and medium calibers. The more demanding artillery tasks require the army's powerful self-propelled guns.

SELF-PROPELLED HOWITZERS

Since World War Two the United States has led the field in converting from towed to self-propelled artillery. At the end of the war in 1945, the Germans had a large number of self-propelled guns in use. These took a heavy toll on the Allied tanks and other armored vehicles. With most tanks fitted with armor designed to protect them against enemy tanks with 75mm guns, it came as a shock to some tank commanders to find themselves faced with a heavy gunned "tank destroyer" wielding an 88mm gun. The only solution was to out-maneuver the big tank destroyer, which could not move as rapidly as the lighter tanks.

After the war, the U.S. Army set to work on development of a 105mm motor gun carriage for self-propelled artillery. In 1951 the M52 went into production and saw service in the **Korean War**. The design had been rushed through, and it still had many problems. These were eventually sorted out, and the M52 was widely deployed. The M52 weighed 26 tons and the vehicle had a traveling range of 280 miles between refueling stops. The gun could fire its shells across a range of seven miles. The vehicle hull carried 102 rounds of ammunition, and the M52 also saw extensive service with the German army.

Armored personnel carriers, light escort cars, and a variety of armored vehicles are required to support artillery units and keep them moving across country.

In 1952 a conference in Washington, D.C., decided that existing United States artillery was not good enough. At this time, American forces were fighting in Korea, and the poor performance of the first few M52s led the generals to order up a new 105mm self-propelled howitzer. It appeared in 1962 as a diesel-powered, 25-ton vehicle with a 105mm gun capable of firing 42-pound shells a distance of seven miles. The M108 chassis incorporated many features built into the M113 armored personnel carrier. With its fully swiveling turret, it was more like a tank than a howitzer.

While the 1952 Washington conference decided a new 105mm howitzer should be produced, it also decided on the need for a new 155mm self-propelled gun, later known as the M109. This piece is still the mainstay of U.S. Army self-propelled artillery and has had an outstandingly successful period of service. The first

The standard British 105mm light gun is capable of firing American 105mm ammunition and has a range of up to 6.8 miles.

prototype was completed in 1959, and it was decided that a diesel engine should be adopted. The gun entered service with the army in 1963, and from 1972 a version with a longer gun has been operational, taking it from 20 to 33 caliber and increasing the range.

The driver sits in front in a special compartment in the fixed hull. Five other crew members are carried in the rotating turret. These include the commander, the gunner, and three ammunition loaders. The driver has a single hatch cover, and in front of it are three small periscopes looking forward. The turret is attached to the rear of the hull, which is 20 feet long and 11 feet wide. It has two doors at the back and a square hatch each side on top. The commander sits to the right of the turret and the gunner sits on the left. Ammunition is supplied through the rear doors.

Although they would be a vital asset in a major war, guns designed to use ammunition from other countries are not at all ▶ *common.*

The M109 self-propelled howitzer, now common in the U.S. Army, had its origins in a 1952 conference held in Washington, D.C., where it was decided there was an urgent need for a new gun of this type. ▼

The M109 has been developed through a series of different versions into a vehicle with a total weight of 27 tons and a top speed of 35 MPH over a range of about 217 miles.

The basic M109 has a 155mm gun just 10 feet long, but capable of firing a standard high-explosive shell a distance of nine miles. Since 1972, the M109A1 version has been fitted with the longer 16.5-foot barrel. With this, the gun can propel its charge a distance of slightly more than twelve miles. A second version, the M109A2, was introduced in 1978. This incorporated improvements made to the basic M109 plus additional safety features and higher reliability.

The combat weight of the M109 is 27 tons, and its total length, including the main gun, is almost 30 feet. The M109 has a total width of 10 feet and a height above the ground of 10 feet, 9 inches. When the gun is prepared for use, a large spade is lowered from the back of the hull to stabilize the vehicle when it fires and prevent it from tipping back. The spade digs into the ground and takes the recoil from the barrel. The M109 uses a General Motors turbo-charged 405 horsepower diesel engine. It gives the M109 a top speed of 35 MPH and a traveling range of about 217 miles.

To support the M109, the army uses a field artillery ammunition support vehicle (**FAASV**). This vehicle is deisgnated the M992 and carries additional ammunition to feed the self-propelled gun. It is similar in appearance to the bottom half of the M109 but has no rotating turret and no gun. Instead, it has a box-shaped structure on top with a crane one end and a shell feeder at the other.

Away from the battlefield is a supply depot where ammunition for the M109 is stored. A crane on the front of the supply unit loads shells and charges into the top of the M992 through a hatch. The hatch is then closed and the driver moves off to rendezvous with the self-propelled gun. He backs up the supply vehicle to the rear of the big gun and opens up the rear door on the supply vehicle. He then attaches a mechanical, motor-driven feeder. It is similar to a conveyor belt, and shells are fed across to the M109 to maintain a continuous rate of fire. The M109 can fire four rounds per minute for the first three minutes and then one round per minute for the next hour.

The field support vehicle is just over 22 feet in length, with a width of 10 feet and a height of 10 feet, 6 inches. It weighs a little over 29 tons and carries a 1.27mm machine gun. The support vehicle has a crew of three and a range of 220 miles at 35 MPH. It can carry 90 rounds of 155mm ammunition and has all the rough country handling characteristics of the M109. The M992 has been deployed in Europe, where it would be used to support mobile operations with the self-propelled gun, creating a truly flexible team of gun and support vehicle.

Some self-propelled M109 guns have been fitted with special protective gear enabling the gun and its crew to keep operating in hazardous battle conditions. These include an environment in which the enemy has fired chemical weapons, is using biological weapons to spread bacteria and harmful organisms, or is using nuclear weapons to spread radiation. The crew would wear special protective clothing, allowing them to stay on the battlefield and continue firing at enemy positions.

The driver of this M109A3 waits in his self-propelled howitzer for the order to move to a new position.

The M109 can cross obstacles up to 1 feet, 9 inches high and cross trenches 6 feet across. It can also ford rivers and streams up to 6 feet deep. Although not used very often, a special flotation kit has been produced. Nine inflatable airbags, usually delivered separately by truck, can be fitted to the vehicle. Four are positioned on each side and one at the front. Outfitted this way, the vehicle can drive into the water and float when the water becomes deep. The rotating tracks propel the vehicle through the water at a steady 4 MPH.

Several countries have purchased the M109 and some, like Italy, South Korea, and the Netherlands have carried out their own limited miodifications. Others, such as Israel, are in the forefront of making major improvements. Under the Howitzer Improvement Program (**HIP**) jointly under way with Israel, the army is looking at the possibility of changing the length of the

Canadian soldiers are given a quick lesson in the functions of the M109A1 howitzer during a combined U.S./Canadian exercise called Rendezvous '83.

M109A2 BASIC LOADS
SOLID vs LIQUID

TOTAL CHARGES 34

**TOTAL CHARGES 34
(M119A1 EQUIVALENT)**

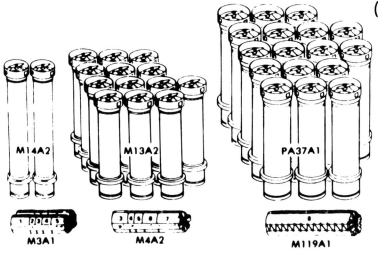

M14A2 M13A2 PA37A1

M3A1 M4A2 M119A1

1 x 55 gal DRUM

JUN 83

Although each M109A2 can carry 34 solid charges, used to propel the shell along the gun barrel, these take up a lot of space. Liquid charges for a new M119 gun could, if used, be carried in a single 55-gallon drum.

PROJECTILE, 155 MM, HE, M483A1
(W/ 88 M 42 / M 46 DP GRENADES)

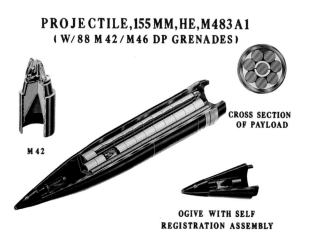

M 42

CROSS SECTION
OF PAYLOAD

OGIVE WITH SELF
REGISTRATION ASSEMBLY

Each shell used by the M109 and other guns is a complex piece of precision engineering, whether used for conventional or ▶ nuclear explosives.

barrel. With the barrel lengthened to 27 feet and other internal improvements, the gun should have a range of 28 miles, a considerable improvement on the present range of 12 miles. In this way the M109 can be made to support wider ranges of duty, including a more important role for bombarding heavy positions and firing anti-tank munitions. These can be mines dropped directly on top of advancing tank columns, or cratering munitions that tear up large areas of concrete.

The M109 is likely to remain in front-line service well into the 1990s and to see service with other armies well into the next century. Nothing is being developed yet to

Developed during the late 1960s, the 175mm M107 self-propelled gun could fire high explosive charges a distance of twenty miles.

replace this howitzer, and several improvements and modifications are likely to appear before it is finally replaced as the mainstay of U.S. Army 155mm artillery. At the end of 1988 the army was operating approximately 2,440 M109 self-propelled guns, which represented almost one-half the total force of towed and self-propelled artillery.

During the 1950s, the standard heavy-field artillery pieces were incapable of being moved by the aircraft of the period. A decision was made to produce heavy howitzers that could be transported by air wherever they were needed. This decision resulted in the 175mm M107

self-propelled gun and the 203mm M110. The M107 weighed 31 tons, and its gun could fire conventional high-explosive charges a maximum distance of twenty miles. A number of problems with the gun were never fully resolved, and the U.S. Army had withdrawn it from use by 1982, just eighteen years after it was first introduced. The M107 was exported to ten countries, including Britain and West Germany, and a few other countries still operate it today.

The top of U.S. Army heavyweight range now is occupied by the M110, a 203mm self-propelled gun capable of propelling a high explosive, rocket-assisted

The M110 weighs more than 31 tons and carries a spade at the
◄ *rear that digs into the ground and prevents it from tipping over*
when the gun is fired.

charge a distance of almost nineteen miles. It can also fire a wide range of conventional and nuclear munitions, including **neutron weapons** that reduce blast but increase the lethal radiation usually associated with atomic charges.

The M110 is 35 feet in length, including the gun and the rear spade that stabilizes the recoil effect of firing this very big howitzer. The M110 weighs more than 31 tons and is driven along by a General Motors turbo-charged diesel engine. It has a top road speed of 34 MPH and an unrefueled range of 325 miles. The M110 is, however, handicapped by the lack of adequate covering or protection for the five crew members that ride with the vehicle — the commander, the gunner, and three loaders. The other eight members of the firing crew ride along separately on a tracked vehicle called M548.

The tracks are supported by five large road wheels to support the weight, a large rear idler wheel of the same diameter at the back, and a small drive wheel connected to the engine transmission at the front. A road wheel is a wheel that is not connected to the engine but helps support the weight of the entire vehicle as it rolls along. An idler wheel carries the track back around the road wheels, and a drive wheel is connected to the engine to pull the tracks around.

The U.S. Army has more than 1,000 M110 heavy howitzers in
◄ *service and these have also been exported to several friendly*
countries.

The gun is officially supposed to fire one round every two minutes but an experienced, well-coordinated gun crew can halve this time for short periods. Because shells for these guns are very heavy, each more than 200 pounds, a special hoist is fitted at the rear to swing the projectile onto the loading tray. The round is then pushed hydraulically into the **breech**. The breech is the block at the base of the barrel where the charge is placed for firing the shell case. The case is then ejected from the back of the breech as the charge flies forward along the barrel. Only two rounds are carried on the gun itself, and additional rounds are supplied by an M548 support vehicle.

At the end of 1988 there were more than 1,000 M110 heavy howitzers in service with the U.S. Army, and the type had also been supplied to several foreign countries. A number of different versions were produced over the years since the M110 first saw duty in 1963, although such a large gun is basically limited by the difficulty of supporting it under conditions of mobile warfare. It represents possibly the last in a long line of heavy howitzers that saw their origins in the massive, unwieldy guns of World War One.

Operating mobile and sometimes fast-moving artillery units means troops must remain constantly on alert for a change in ▶ position; it also means living in tents.

Artillery pieces, their support trucks, and essential vehicles are usually designed to fit inside standard transport planes. ▼

ON THE BATTLEFIELD

Constant training by U.S. artillery troops maintains the force at a high level of combat readiness. ▲

As we saw in the first section of this book, artillery has been the greatest cause of human casualties in every major war in this century, and it remains an important part of any modern conflict. It can cause devastating damage upon the enemy, and it can also be used to support almost every action the friendly forces are called upon to perform. The first and foremost job of the artillery is fire assault. This is designed to destroy enemy supplies, fixed command posts, or infantry. Next, harassing fire is used to cause confusion in the enemy ranks and to create a feeling of uncertainty as to which positions are safe and which are threatened.

Tactical use of artillery usually fills two objectives. The first is to strike the rear areas of the battlefield, causing chaos in the supply lines and back-up troops moving to the front line. The second objective is to give direct support to friendly units maneuvering to attack. This is done by concentrating fire on enemy gun positions to prevent them from attacking armored personnel carriers bringing up the ground troops. Guns and howitzers are used within about twenty miles of the forward line of action, called the **FLOT**. Beyond the FLOT, missiles and rockets are used to strike targets farther away.

◄ *Soviet artillery troops train to fight under all conditions and across all kinds of countryside.*

The army puts its artillery into action within groups called divisions. Each division has 2,500 personnel. Each 155mm battalion supports one of the division's brigades and has six guns. The battalion sends men forward toward the target and they report back on how accurate the gunners are. These men move forward with the infantry and call back to the gun sites by radio. When the time comes for the gun sites to move forward, artillery battalions move in cooperative pairs. That is, one half, with three guns, stays fixed and fires its guns to cover the forward movement of the second battalion that packs

A laser-guided cannon-launched projectile is fired from an M198 during testing at White Sands Missile Range, New Mexico.

up its guns and advances. Then that group of three guns fixes, fires, and covers the other three as they, too, move forward.

If a major war ever broke out and the army found itself fighting a heavy artillery action, it would be faced with fierce opposition. The enemy knows the damage guns and howitzers can cause, and they would be just as determined as U.S. commanders to gain control through heavy bombardment. Soviet ground forces operate about 29,000 pieces of artillery, of which 5,000 are self-propelled guns. This compares with about 5,700 pieces of artillery in the U.S. Army, of which about 2,500 are self-propelled. The most powerful Soviet self-propelled gun is the 203mm 2S7, but one of the most advanced is the 2S5 with a 152mm gun and a range of twenty-five miles using high-explosive shells. The 2S7 is based on the 2S5 and they are a formidable pair of guns for a highly mobile war. Like the Americans, Soviet army commanders know the awesome potential of the self-propelled gun.

An M198 towed howitzer fires a high-angle shot.

ABBREVIATIONS

FAASV   Field Artillery Ammunition Support Vehicle

FLOT   Forward Line of Action

HIP   Howitzer Improvement Program

GLOSSARY

Armored personnel carriers	Tracked or wheeled vehicles protected with armor plate and used to carry soldiers or infantry men.
Artillery	Fixed or mobile guns and cannons pulled by powered vehicles or fitted with an engine for self-propulsion.
Breech	A block at the base of the barrel of the gun where the charge is placed for firing from the shell case.
Caliber	The diameter of the inside of the barrel of a gun usually indicating the power of the artillery piece.
Howitzers	Large guns and cannons that have short barrels for firing low-speed charges.
Korean War	A war between 1950 and 1953 in which the United States repelled North Korean communist forces from invading South Korea.
Muzzle	The front end of a gun barrel.
Neutron weapons	Nuclear weapons designed to minimize the blast effect but produce high levels of radiation for killing people rather than destroying buildings.
North Atlantic Treaty Organization (NATO)	An alliance of the U.S., Canada, and 11 West European countries operating under a military pact to support one another; an attack on one is considered an attack on all.
Rocket-assisted shells	Shells containing small rocket motors in the rear casing to propel them beyond the normal range of the gun.
Self-propelled artillery	Guns, cannons, or howitzers that carry their own mode of propulsion and therefore do not have to be towed.
Vietnam War	A conflict in Vietnam in which the U.S. armed forces assisted the national forces of the government of South Vietnam until it was overrun by communist North Vietnam in the early 1970s.

INDEX

Page references in *italics* indicate photographs or illustrations.